CW00968283

Happy Christmas, God

Copyright ⓒ 1990 Éditions du Centurion/Bayard Presse
Translation copyright ⓒ 1991 Lion Publishing plc

Published by
Lion Publishing plc
Sandy Lane West, Oxford, England
ISBN 0 7459 2238 4
Lion Publishing Corporation
1705 Hubbard Avenue, Batavia, Illinois 60510, USA
ISBN 0 7459 2238 4
Albatross Books Pty Ltd
PO Box 320, Sutherland, NSW 2232, Australia
ISBN 0 7324 0532 7

First published 1990 by Éditions du Centurion/Bayard Presse under the title
of *Images pour prier à Noël*
First English edition published 1991 by Lion Publishing plc

British Library CIP data and Library of Congress CIP data applied for

Printed in France

Impression et reliure : Pollina s.a., 85400 Luçon - n° 13956

My Picture Prayer Book

Happy Christmas, God

Marie Aubinais
Illustrations by Dominique Thibault

A LION BOOK
Oxford · Batavia · Sydney

Preface

Christmas is a very special time for children. The whispered secrets and the long-awaited surprises are a source of great excitement to them. They enjoy the busy, fun-filled days. And they love to hear the story of a baby who was just like them, and yet who came to change the world.

Today it's impossible to separate Christmas from its trappings. They are bound together so much that Christmas festivities and religious celebration are part and parcel of the same thing.

Children respond most readily to the things they can experience, see and touch. This book is designed to help children see beyond the presents and decorations and to remind them of the real meaning of the festival.

Prayer itself is a journey from outer things to inner reality. The final picture, of a starry sky, points to God's infinite greatness, which in turn leads to a real joy in living.

Christmas is
a great big party

Christmas is a very special time:
there's so much to look forward to,
so much fun.
And it's all because of God,
who came to this world
as a little baby.

You can tell that Christmas is coming
when you see Christmas trees
and Christmas lights,
and you have parties and presents.

The next four pictures
are to help you talk to God
in the midst of the Christmas fun.

The Christmas tree

The Christmas tree's leaves
stay green and bright
even when winter days are grey
and snow turns the whole world white.
The tree shows that it is still alive
when the rest of nature is sleeping.

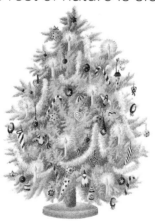

Dear God,
you give life to the world.

Christmas lights

Christmas lights
shine and sparkle all around.
The lights in every window
cheer the passers by.
Outdoor lights
cast their beams far and wide.
They light up the world
making it happy and bright.

Dear God,
you give light to the world.

Parties

Christmas is a time for parties!
People make long journeys
to be with those they love.
They talk, and laugh, and eat,
and sing, and play games,
and dance.
It's so nice to be together!
If only these times could last
forever.

*Dear God,
you give joy to the world.*

Presents

Christmas is a time for presents.
Giving presents is a bit like
hugging someone you like.
One person gives
and the other receives
because they love each other.
You can see the gift
even though you can't see the love.

*Dear God, at Christmas time,
you give yourself
as a gift to the world.*

Christmas is
a special feeling inside

Christmas is a special time
when God comes.
The church bells
ring from their towers,
making hearts beat faster
with excitement.
When Christmas bells ring out
on Christmas night
people feel happy inside.

The next four pictures
are to help you to pray
when you get that Christmas feeling.

Waiting

Christmas seems to come
so slowly.
You can count the days
as you open the windows
on an Advent calendar.
It is a bit like walking
step by step
up a long, long stairway
to the light.

Dear God,
I look forward to your coming.
I am waiting for you.

Peace

At Christmas time
peace comes to the earth
like big, soft snowflakes.
Quarrelling,
fighting,
and even war
cease
for just a moment.

*Dear God, you alone
can help us make peace.*

Love

Christmas is like a giant bonfire
warming the world
and all the people who live in it.
Christmas brings a special warmth
that could melt
cold, evil, fear,
and everything that is hard
and unkind
in the hearts of people.

*Dear God, you alone
give the love that warms me.*

23

A new beginning

Christmas is like a clear morning
and the promise of a bright new day.
After days of waiting
Christmas has come at last,
and something special
is about to happen.
The world seems sparkling and new
and full of hope.

Dear God, at Christmas
I realize how special you are.

Christmas is
a time of waiting

At Christmas time,
God comes to the world.
Long, long years ago
many people who believed in God
waited for him to come.
Patiently, joyfully,
they waited for a special king.
Their poems tell us their story.

The next four poems
are ones they used
to help them think about God
as they waited for him to come.

Thirst

O God, you are my God,
I am trying so hard to find you;
without you, I feel as thirsty and alone
as a wanderer lost in the desert.

Psalm 63

Dear God, I long for you.
Just as my body needs water,
so I need you.

Patience

As the soil
makes the young plants grow,
and as seeds unfold
in a garden,
so will God make goodness
and songs of praise
spring up in all the world.

Isaiah 61:11

*Just as the soil
makes the young plants grow,
I want to get ready
for you to come, dear God.*

Joy

Let the world rejoice:
the skies, the seas, the land.
Let all living things rejoice:
the plants, the animals,
the forest trees.
The whole world should sing aloud
for God is coming!

Psalm 96:11-13

*Let the whole world rejoice
for you are coming, dear God!*

Here at last!

Open up, open up,
O doors, open up.
Let the glorious king come in.
Who is this glorious king?
It is God himself,
strong and powerful,
the God who wins every battle.

Psalm 24

Dear God, your only crown
was made of thorns.
Are you the mighty king
your people longed for?

Christmas is
God coming to us

On the first Christmas Day
God came to this world.
The scene by the manger
tells the story of his coming.
God became a tiny baby,
born in a room where animals lived.
Shepherds came to see him,
and wise men from distant lands.
Our Christmas celebrations
are to welcome him as king.

The next four pictures
are to help you to pray
to God who became a human being.

A baby

Joseph and Mary lived in Nazareth.
Mary was expecting a baby.
One day, Joseph and Mary
had to go to Bethlehem.
While they were there
their baby was born.
It was a little baby boy
called Jesus.

Dear Jesus, you are special,
for you came as a tiny baby
to an ordinary mother
even though you are God.

The shepherds

Mary and Joseph had to stay
with the animals,
because there was no room
for them in the house.
Mary put her baby, Jesus,
in a manger to sleep.
Angels from heaven
told shepherds the news of his birth
and they came to see him.

Dear Jesus, you are special,
for you were born
in an ordinary home
yet you came to change the world.

41

The wise men

The wise men lived far, far away.
One day, as they studied the stars,
they saw a sign
that a king had been born.
They had to travel a long way
to visit him.
When they reached Jesus,
they knelt down
and gave him gifts.

Dear Jesus, you are special,
for you came
to all the people of the world.

Jesus, son of God

God came to earth as Jesus.
He came as a tiny baby,
he grew up,
he spent his life doing good,
he died and came to life again.
His new life means that we too
can have new life.
He has rescued us.

*Dear Jesus, you are special,
for you are the true light
and you came to this world
to bring light to all people.*

How this book works

Section 1: We think of Christmas first as a party. Here are four pictures of familiar Christmas trimmings that each say something about what God is like, even though we cannot see him: **the Christmas tree**, page 8; **Christmas lights**, page 10; **parties**, page 12; **presents**, page 14.

Section 2: Christmas stirs up deep feelings. It is a season when people take the time to show affection for each other, and old quarrels are forgotten. Here are four pictures that say something about the deeper meaning of Christmas: the way individuals change when God comes to them: **waiting,** page 18; **peace**, page 20; **love**, page 22; **a new beginning**, page 24.

Section 3: Prayer is also a way of linking ourselves with people who have prayed in other times or in other places. Here are four pictures to help children recognize this dimension of prayer with words from four passages in the Old Testament. They reflect the blend of confidence and uncertainty in waiting for something important that children will recognize easily to happen: **thirst,**

Section 4: The nativity story is central to Christmas. Here are four pictures that tell the story and show how an apparently insignificant birth is the source of eternal hope:

How to use this book with children

The simplest way is to work through the book from beginning to end, stopping to look and read where the child shows interest. Or you might like to use it as a way of leading up to Christmas through the days of Advent.

Yet another way would be to dip into it regularly, using a familiar, relevant starting point. For example, a child who has just received a gift will understand the imagery of a present. A child who has the opportunity to see a newborn baby will marvel even more at the picture of the baby Jesus. The picture about waiting will be helpful if Christmas seems a long time coming.

Gradually, children will learn how to choose the picture that best suits their mood or what is going on in their life. Tiny details in pictures can sometimes provide a great deal of spiritual insight.

It is hoped that this book will help children to celebrate the festival of Christmas; and more than that, to understand the meaning of Christmas, which can make every day of their life a celebration.